dog names

dog names

Jenny Linford

RYLAND
PETERS
& SMALL

LONDON NEW YORK

Designer Iona Hoyle
Senior Editor Miriam Hyslop
Picture Researcher Emily Westlake
Production Gordana Simakovic
Art Director Anne-Marie Bulat
Publishing Director Alison Starling

First published in the United States in 2006
by Ryland Peters & Small, Inc.
519 Broadway, 5th Floor
New York, NY 10012
www.rylandpeters.com

10 9 8 7 6 5 4 3 2 1

Text, design, and photography
© Ryland Peters & Small 2006

ISBN-10: 1-84597-272-4
ISBN-13: 978-1-84597-272-1

Printed and bound in China

contents

introduction

Bringing home a small puppy is one of life's great pleasures. Owning a new puppy, however, does bring with it a particular dilemma. What should this endearing little creature be called? It's so important to find a name that you really like (bearing in mind that you will have to call to your dog in public!) and which suits your new canine companion. While, of course, classic names like Dog or Scruff continue to be popular, there is a rich seam of possible dog names to mine. Choose from names that reflect your dog's coloring and markings, like Jet, Spot, or Whiskey, or its personality, like Caesar for commanding dogs or Frisky for lively canines. Alternatively, name your puppy after famous fictional or real-life canines such as Lassie or Tintin's Snowy. With over 1,000 names to choose from, naming your new puppy has never been so easy or so much fun.

classic dogs

Angus
An old-fashioned Scottish name for male dogs.

Animal
A fundamental name for dogs.

Atom
For small, fast-moving dogs of either sex.

Bach
A music-inspired, punning name for vocal dogs.

Bali
A tropical name for mellow dogs of either sex.

Baloo
For large, friendly dogs, after the bear in *The Jungle Book*.

Banana
A fruit-inspired name for dogs.

Banjo
A music-inspired name for vocal dogs.

Barker
For noisy male dogs.

Baskerville
For huge hounds, after Sir Arthur Conan Doyle's creation *The Hound of the Baskervilles*.

Beachcomber
For male dogs who enjoy finding things.

Bear
For large, bear-like dogs.

Beau
For attractive dogs; from the French for "handsome."

Big
A simple name for large dogs.

Bingo
For lucky dogs; after the game.

Blade
For sleek dogs of either sex.

Blue
A popular name for dogs of either sex and any color.

Bolero
A musical name for vocal dogs.

Bonkers
An affectionate name for nutty dogs.

Bono
For bone-loving canines.

Bonzo
A classic male dog name.

Boo
For surprising dogs of either sex.

Boomerang
For dogs that are good at returning to their owners.

Booster
For energetic male dogs.

Boots
For dogs with distinctive-colored paws.

Bouncer
A simple name for lively dogs.

Bow
An endearing name for canines.

Bubbles
For cheerful, light-hearted dogs of either sex.

Buddy
A classic name for friendly male dogs.

Bug
A cheery, insect-inspired name for dogs of either sex.

Bumble
An affectionate name for slow-moving dogs.

Burger
A food-inspired name for greedy dogs.

Buster
A classic name for friendly male dogs.

Butch
Traditional name for tough dogs.

Butterball
An affectionate name for chubby dogs of either sex.

Buttons
For bright-eyed dogs.

Buzz
For speedy dogs of either sex.

Capricorn
A Zodiac-inspired name for nimble-footed dogs.

Cello
A music-inspired name for vocal dogs.

Challenger
For male dogs who enjoy a challenge.

Chewbacca
A *Star Wars*-inspired name for large, hairy dogs.

Chewy
For dogs who can't resist getting their teeth into things.

Chianti
A wine-inspired name for dogs of either sex.

Chips
A down-to-earth name for food-loving dogs.

Chowder
A food-inspired name for greedy dogs.

Chum
A traditional name for friendly male dogs.

Chutney
A relish-inspired name for dogs of either sex.

Clown
For dogs with a sense of humor.

Comet
An astrological name for dogs of either sex.

Couscous
For greedy dogs of either sex; after the North African staple.

Coyote
After the wild wolf.

Cracker
A cheerful, food-inspired name for dogs of either sex.

Cranberry
A fruit-inspired name for dogs of either sex.

Crash
For clumsy male dogs.

Crumpet
A humorous, food-inspired name for greedy dogs.

Cruncher
For dogs who enjoy chewing bones.

Crusher
For strong, tough male dogs.

Dandy
For elegant male dogs.

Dart
For fast-moving dogs of either sex.

Dash
For dogs that like to run around.

Dawn
For early-rising female dogs.

Delicious
For food-loving dogs of either sex.

Digger
For dogs who can't resist a bit of digging.

Dingo
After the Australian wild dog.

Dino
For large dogs; abbreviated from "dinosaur."

Dog
A fundamental canine name.

Doggle
An affectionate name for lively dogs of either sex.

Doodle
An endearing name for dogs of either sex.

Doughnut
A cheery name for greedy dogs.

Dumbo
For large gray dogs, after Disney's lovable elephant.

Dumpling
An affectionate name for rotund dogs.

Dynamite
For explosive male dogs.

Elvis
A rock 'n' roll name for music-loving hound dogs.

E.T.
An extraterrestrial name for lovable dogs.

Fang
For sharp-toothed dogs.

Fatso
A humorous name for portly dogs.

Fetch
A classic dog name for dogs that enjoy retrieving sticks for their owners.

Fidget
For small, restless dogs.

Fido
A classic male dog name.

Flapjack
A food-inspired name for greedy male dogs.

Flea
An affectionate name for small dogs.

Flip-flop
For mellow dogs of either sex.

classic dogs

11

Football
For dogs who love to play with balls.

Frisbee
A game-inspired name.

Fungus
A food-inspired name for dogs of either sex.

Galaxy
An apt name for large dogs.

Gale
For dogs who enjoy wild weather.

Garlic
A food-inspired name for dogs.

Genie
For dogs of either sex.

Gobble
For greedy dogs of either sex.

Goliath
For large, male dogs.

Gremlin
For dogs that cause all sorts of trouble.

Growler
For intimidating male guard dogs.

Gucci
For fashionable dogs of either sex; after the Italian fashion house.

Gulper
For greedy male dogs.

Gumdrop
A humorous name for dogs of either sex.

Gypsy
For wandering canines.

Heinz
For mongrels, after Heinz's "57 Varieties."

Helix
A DNA-inspired name for dogs of either sex.

Hobbit
A *The Lord of the Rings*-inspired name for small furry dogs.

Horse
A popular name for large, strong dogs.

Hot Dog
A food-inspired name for greedy dogs.

Howl
For dogs who enjoy howling at the moon (or the mailman).

Hunter
A classic name for good hunting dogs.

Hurricane
For enthusiastic, energetic canines that leave a trail of destruction in their path.

Jabberwocky
A humorous name, from Lewis Carroll's poem.

Jambalaya
A food-inspired name for greedy dogs.

Jaws
For large-mouthed, sharp-toothed dogs.

Jelly
A humorous name for nervous dogs of either sex.

Jellybean
An endearing name for loveable, sweet-natured canines of either sex.

Jimbob
A humorous name for male dogs, after the character in TV series *The Waltons*.

Jitterbug
A dance-inspired name for dogs of either sex.

K-9
A punning, robotic name for canines.

Ki
A classic French name, from the Breton for "dog."

Killer
A classic name for savage, feral dogs of either sex.

King
A popular name for regal male canines.

Lamb
For sweet-tempered, gentle dogs of either sex.

Leviathan
A biblical name for large, imposing dogs.

London
A capital name for city-living dogs.

Lucky
An affectionate name for dogs of either sex.

Macintosh
For dogs who enjoy getting wet; after the waterproof raincoat.

Magic
A name for dogs of either sex.

Meatball
For large dogs with a healthy appetite.

Meatloaf
A food-inspired name for greedy male dogs.

Mighty
For big, strong male dogs.

Milkshake
A drink-inspired name for thirsty dogs of either sex.

Mini
For small female dogs.

Miss
A classic name for female dogs.

Mister
A classic name for male dogs.

Misto
From the Italian for "mixed;" ideal for mongrels.

Molecule
For small dogs of either sex.

Mopsy
For small, very hairy dogs of either sex.

Muddles
An affectionate name for confused dogs.

Muddy
A self-explanatory name for dogs who enjoy getting dirty.

Mungo
A classic name for male dogs.

Mutt
A down-to-earth name for dogs.

Nantucket
For dogs who enjoy having a whale of a time; after the island with its history of whaling.

Navigator
For dogs who are good at finding the way.

Nemo
For water-loving male dogs; after Jules Verne's literary creation Captain Nemo.

Neutron
A molecule-inspired name for small dogs of either sex.

Nibbler
For dogs of either sex who just can't resist a nibble.

Nipper
For male dogs with a tendency to nip.

Nippy
For quick and nimble dogs of either sex.

Nomad
For wandering dogs of either sex.

Nutmeg
A spice-inspired name for dogs of either sex.

Parma
A food-inspired name—after Italian Parma ham—for dogs who enjoy fine food.

Paws
A classic dog's name.

Pesto
A food-inspired name for dogs of either sex.

Pickles
For naughty canines that often find themselves in trouble.

Piglet
An affectionate name for small, greedy dogs of either sex.

Pirate
For male dogs with a tendency to steal things.

Pixie
For small, enchanting dogs of either sex.

Podge
A humorous name for chubby dogs of either sex.

Pudding
A food-inspired name for sweet dogs of either sex.

Pup
A traditional name for youthful canines.

Quince
A fruit-inspired name for dogs of either sex.

Racer
For fast-moving dogs.

Radar
For dogs who are good at finding their way.

Rags
An old-fashioned dog name.

Ragu
A food-inspired name for greedy male dogs.

Rambler
For dogs who enjoy long, leisurely strolls.

Ranger
For outdoor-loving dogs.

Ravioli
A pasta-inspired name for food-loving dogs.

Regalo
From the Italian for "present," for dogs who are gifts.

Ricochet
For speedy, all-over-the-place hounds.

Rocket
For fast-moving male dogs.

Roly-Poly
A cheerful, affectionate name for chubby dogs.

Roma
A cosmopolitan name for city dogs; after the Italian capital.

Roo
A marsupial-inspired name for high-jumping dogs.

Rover
For dogs who like to explore.

Ruff
A classic name for male dogs.

Rugrat
Inspired by the children's cartoon series.

Runt
For small dogs, or the runt of the litter.

Safari
For adventurous dogs who enjoy long journeys.

Salsa
A dance-inspired name for rhythmic dogs of either sex.

Sandwich
A fun, food-inspired name
for greedy dogs.

Sausage
An affectionate name for
small dogs.

Scallywag
For sassy male dogs.

Scrabble
A game-inspired name for dogs
of either sex.

Scrap
For small, scruffy dogs.

Scruff
For endearingly messy dogs.

Sesame
A food-inspired name for dogs
of either sex.

Shadow
For dogs of either sex who like to
follow their owner.

Shaggy
An affectionate name for
hairy dogs.

Shrimp
An endearing name for small
dogs of either sex.

Sirius
For male dogs, after Sirius the
dog star.

Skip
A cheerful, monosyllabic name.

Sky
For graceful dogs, especially
blue-gray ones.

Slipper
For dogs with a taste for
footwear.

Smiffy
An endearing name.

Smudge
For messy dogs of either sex.

Snappy
For bad-tempered dogs.

Sniff
For dogs who like sniffing about.

Snuff
A humorous name for male
canines.

Snufkin
An endearing name for male
dogs; from *The Moomins*.

Snuffles
For dogs who enjoy sniffing.

Socks
For dogs with distinctive
markings on their paws.

Sparky
For bright, lively dogs.

Spike
A classic dog name.

Spitfire
For speedy dogs.

Sprocket
A humorous name for
male dogs.

classic dogs

15

Sputnik
A space-inspired name for male dogs; after the world's first artificial satellite.

Squeak
For small-voiced dogs of either sex.

Star
For bright-eyed, night-loving dogs of either sex.

Strider
For long-legged dogs who enjoy going for walks.

Sumo
For large dogs; after the Japanese wrestlers.

Superdog
For wonder-dogs that always save the day.

Talisman
For lucky dogs of either sex.

Terminator
For formidable male dogs.

Thimble
A classic name for small dogs.

Thor
For loud-barking dogs; after the Norse god of thunder.

Titch
An affectionate name for small dogs.

Toggles
A humorous name for dogs of either sex.

Truffle
A food-inspired name for gourmet male dogs.

Tucker
For greedy dogs of either sex.

Uncle
A family-inspired name.

Waddle
A humorous name for slow-moving dogs.

Waffle
A food-inspired name for greedy dogs of either sex.

Walrus
An expressive name for large, heavy dogs.

Wookiee
A *Star Wars*-inspired name for large, hairy dogs.

Wriggle
A humorous name for fidgety, wriggly dogs.

Yap
For dogs that bark a lot.

Yoga
For mellow, deep-breathing dogs of either sex.

Yogi
For bearlike dogs, after cartoon character Yogi Bear.

Zen
For philosophic dogs.

Zigzag
For dogs that run all over the place.

Zippy
For speedy dogs of either sex.

Zoom
For fast-running dogs.

pedigree dogs

Alaska
For thick-furred, snow-loving dogs, such as Huskies.

Ali
For Boxers, after champion boxer Muhammad Ali.

Aztec
A Mexican-inspired name for Chihuahuas.

Babushka
A female name for Russian dogs, such as Borzoi.

Balzac
A literary name for Poodles; after the French novelist.

Bernard
A classic name for St. Bernards.

Blaze
A good name for Red Setters.

Blizzard
A suitable name for snow-loving dogs such as St. Bernards, Alaskan Malamute, or Siberian Huskies.

Bluebird
For speedy dogs such as Greyhounds and Whippets; after the racing car.

Boatswain
For Newfoundland dogs, after Lord Byron's beloved Newfoundland Boatswain.

Bodger
For Bull Terriers, after the old, tough dog in Sheila Burnford's *The Incredible Journey*.

Bonbon
For sweet-tempered Poodles, from the French for "sweet."

Boris
An aristocratic name for Borzois.

Brenin
For regal male Welsh Terriers, from the Welsh for "king."

Brunhilde
A Wagnerian name for female German Shepherds.

Burgundy
A wine-inspired name for Red Setters.

Cameron
A traditional name for Scottish Terriers.

Campbell
For speedy dogs such as Whippets or Greyhounds; after racing driver Donald Campbell.

Cari
An affectionate name for female Welsh Terriers, from the Welsh for "love."

Cassius
For Boxers, after acclaimed boxer Cassius Clay.

Cheetah
For speedy dogs, such as Greyhounds or Whippets.